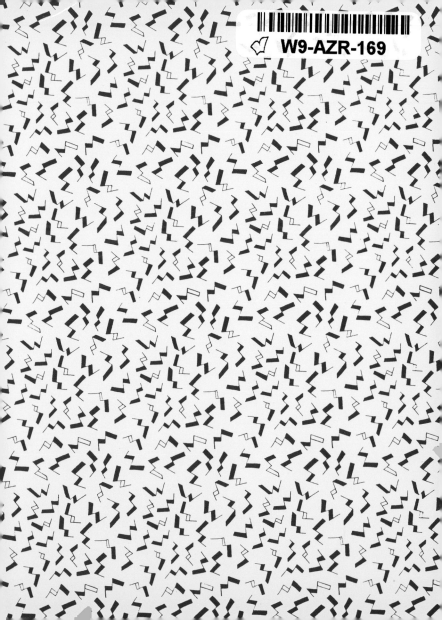

SPEAKING
FOR
OURSELVES

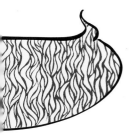

Women's Wit and Wisdom

Ariel Books
Andrews and McMeel
Kansas City

SPEAKING FOR OURSELVES

Edited by Susan Kiley

Illustrated by Lisa Valenti

Book design by Maura Fadden Rosenthal

ISBN: 0-8362-4721-3

Library of Congress Catalog Card Number: 94-71135

introduction

The words of women—our mothers, sisters, daughters, and friends—hold a special place in our hearts. Women's words can comfort and soothe, or they might amuse us, bringing laughter at just the right moment. Sometimes a conversation with another woman will inspire us to action or cause us to view a situation in an unexpected way—or even bring us to a new and startling realization about ourselves.

The quotes in this thoughtful book will bring on not only laughter but also a smile in appreciation of a truth that may have eluded less keen observers of life. Through humorous or poignant observations, the words of women collected here will lift your heart and provide a perspective on the world that only another woman can offer.

Life

What do we live for, if it is not to make life less difficult for each other?
—GEORGE ELIOT

It has begun to occur to me that life is a stage I'm going through.
—ELLEN GOODMAN

One's life has value so long as one attributes value to the life of others, by means of love, friendship, indignation and compassion.
—SIMONE DE BEAUVOIR

Life is something to do when you can't get to sleep.

—FRAN LEBOWITZ

Life is better than death, I believe, if only because it is less boring, and because it has fresh peaches in it.

—Alice Walker

Life, for all its agonies of despair and loss and guilt, is exciting and beautiful, amusing and artful and endearing, full of liking and love, at times a poem and a high adventure, at times noble and at times very gay; and whatever (if anything) is to come after it—we shall not have this life again.

—ROSE MACAULAY

The dedicated life is the life worth living. You must give with your whole heart.

—ANNIE DILLARD

The way I see it, if you want the rainbow, you gotta put up with the rain.
—Dolly Parton

I think of birth as the search for a larger apartment.
—Rita Mae Brown

Expecting life to treat you well because you are a good person is like expecting an angry bull not to charge because you are a vegetarian.
—Shari R. Barr

All my life I've wanted to be somebody.
But I see now I should have been more specific.
—Jane Wagner

Life in the twentieth century is like a parachute jump: you have to get it right the first time.
—Margaret Mead

Women

Woman must not accept; she must challenge. She must not be awed by that which has been built up around her; she must reverence that woman in her which struggles for expression.

—MARGARET SANGER

A liberated woman is one who has sex before marriage and a job after.

—GLORIA STEINEM

Any woman who has a great deal to offer the world is in trouble.
—HAZEL SCOTT

**There is no female mind. The brain is not an organ of sex.
Might as well speak of a female liver.**
—CHARLOTTE PERKINS GILMAN

I have a brain and a uterus, and I use both.
—PATRICIA SCHROEDER

I'm just a person trapped inside a woman's body.
—ELAINE BOOSLER

Women's place is in the House—and in the Senate.
—GLORIA SCHAFFER

Being powerful is like being a lady. If you have to tell people you
are, you aren't.
—MARGARET THATCHER

**The people I'm furious with are the women's
liberationists. They keep getting up on soapboxes and
proclaiming that women are brighter than men. It's true
but it should be kept quiet or it ruins the whole racket.**

—ANITA LOOS

When Harvard men say they have
graduated from Radcliffe, then we've
made it.

—JACQUELINE KENNEDY ONASSIS

**The thing women have got to learn is that nobody
gives you power. You just take it.**

—ROSEANNE ARNOLD

Men are too emotional to vote.
Their conduct at baseball games and
political conventions shows this,
while their innate tendency to appeal
to force renders them particularly
unfit for the task of government.

— ALICE DUER MILLER

What's with you men? Would hair stop growing on your chest if you asked
directions somewhere?
–Erma Bombeck

Giving a man space is like giving a dog a computer:
Chances are he will not use it wisely.
—Bette-Jane Raphael

If men had to have babies they would only ever have one each.
—Princess Diana

If men can run the world, why can't they stop wearing neckties? How intelligent is it to start the day by tying a little noose around your neck?

—Linda Ellerbee

The story of a love is not important—
what is important is that one is capable
of love. It is perhaps the only glimpse
we are permitted of eternity.

—HELEN HAYES

We can only learn to love by loving.
—IRIS MURDOCH

i love you no matter what you do, but do you have to do so much of it?
—JEAN ILLSLEY CLARKE

Relationship is a pervading and changing mystery. . . . Brutal or lovely, the mystery waits for people wherever they go, whatever extreme they run to.

—EUDORA WELTY

Love requires respect and friendship as well as passion. Because there comes a time when you have to get out of bed.

—ERICA JONG

If love is the answer, could you rephrase the question?

—LiLy ToMLiN

No partner in a love relationship . . . should feel that he has to give up an essential part of himself to make it viable.

—MAY SARTON

Fond as we are of our loved ones, there comes at times during their absence an unexplained peace.

—ANNE SHAW

Jealousy is like a hot pepper. Use it mildly, and you add spice to the relationship. Use too much of it and it can burn.

—Ayala M. Pines

It's useless to hold a person to anything he says while he's in love, drunk, or running for office.

—Shirley MacLaine

I'm suggesting we call sex something else, and it should include everything from kissing to sitting close together.

—Shere Hite

A kiss is a lovely trick designed by nature to stop speech when words become superfluous.

—Ingrid Bergman

I have never quite understood this sex symbol business, but if I'm going to be a symbol of something, I'd rather have it sex than some of the other things they've got symbols for.

—Marilyn Monroe

Sex appeal is fifty percent what you've got and fifty percent what people think you've got.

—Sophia Loren

One of my theories is that men love with their eyes; women love with their ears.

—Zsa Zsa Gabor

Work

There is only one woman I know of who could never be a symphony conductor, and that's the VENUS DE MILO.

—MARGARET HILLIS

Every woman is a human being—one cannot repeat that too often—and a human being must have occupation if he or she is not to become a nuisance to the world.

—DOROTHY SAYERS

One never notices what has been done; one can only see what remains to be done.
—MARIE CURIE

My grandfather once told me that there were two kinds of people: those who do the work and those who take the credit. He told me to try to be in the first group; there was much less competition.

—INDIRA GANDHI

We need love and creative imagination to do constructive work.

–PAULA OLLENDORF

Laziness may appear attractive, but work gives satisfaction.

—ANNE FRANK

The simple idea that everyone needs a reasonable amount of challenging work in his or her life, and also a noncompetitive leisure, has never really taken hold.

—JUDITH MARTIN

I remember mentioning the baby-sitter in a column once and receiving outraged letters from readers who could not understand how anyone who could write feelingly of her children would hire help with their care. When did those people think I was writing? In the checkout line at the supermarket?

—ANNA QUINDLEN

Social Graces

The real art of conversation is not only to say the right thing in the right place but to leave unsaid the wrong thing at the tempting moment.

—DOROTHY NEVILL

We are so vain that we even care for the opinion of those we don't care for.

—MARIE VON EBNER-ESCHENBACH

Manners are a sensitive awareness of the feelings of others. If you have that awareness, you have good manners, no matter what fork you use.

—EMILY POST

It is bad manners to contradict a guest. You must never insult people in your own house—always go to theirs.

—MYRTLE REED

Civility costs nothing, and buys everything.

—LADY MARY WORTLEY MONTAGU

Being popular is important. Otherwise people might not like you.

—MIMI POND

A lady is one who never shows her underwear unintentionally.

—LILLIAN DAY

Food

Whenever you see food beautifully arranged on a plate, you know someone's fingers have been all over it.

—Julia Child

If you have formed the habit of checking on every new diet that comes along, you will find that, mercifully, they all blur together, leaving you with only one definite piece of information: french-fried potatoes are out.

—Jean Kerr

As for butter versus margarine, I trust cows more than chemists.

—Joan Gussow

Much serious thought has been devoted to the subject of chocolate: What does chocolate mean? Is the pursuit of chocolate a right or a privilege? Does the notion of chocolate preclude the concept of free will?

—SANDRA BOYNTON

Housework

Housekeeping ain't no joke.

—LOUISA MAY ALCOTT

i hate housework! You make the beds, you do the dishes—and six months later you have to start all over again.

—JOAN RIVERS

I would rather lie on a sofa than sweep beneath it.

—SHIRLEY CONRAN

Housework is the hardest work in the world. That's why men won't do it.

—EDNA FERBER

Beauty

I'm tired of all this nonsense about beauty being only skin-deep.
That's deep enough. What do you want, an adorable pancreas?

—JEAN KERR

**Cosmetics is a boon to every woman, but a girl's best
beauty aid is still a nearsighted man.**
—YOKO ONO

If truth is beauty, how come no one has their hair done in a library?

—LILY TOMLIN

It matters more what's in a woman's face than what's on it

—CLAUDETTE COLBERT

You'd be surprised how much it costs to look this cheap.

—DOLLY PARTON

Women should try to increase their size rather than decrease it, because I believe the bigger we are, the more space we'll take up, and the more we'll have to be reckoned with. I think every woman should be fat like me.

—ROSEANNE ARNOLD

Marriage

Marriage is a great institution, but I'm not ready for an institution, yet.
—MAE WEST

A successful marriage requires falling in love many times, always with the same person.
—MIGNON MCLAUGHLIN

If you want to sacrifice the admiration of many men for the criticism of one, go ahead, get married.

—KATHARINE HEPBURN

Sexiness wears thin after a while, and beauty fades, but to be married to a man who makes you laugh every day, ah, now that's a real treat!

—JOANNE WOODWARD

If love means never having to say you're sorry, then marriage means always having to say everything twice.

—ESTELLE GETTY

In a successful marriage, there is no such thing as one's way. There is only the way of both, only the bumpy, dusty, difficult, but always mutual path!

—PHYLLIS McGINLEY

The long-term accommodation that protects marriage and other such relationships is . . . forgetfulness.

—ALICE WALKER

Positive Reinforcement is hugging your husband when he does a load of laundry. Negative Reinforcement is telling him he used too much detergent.

—DR. JOYCE BROTHERS

It's a waste of time trying to change a man's character. You have to accept your husband as he is.

—QUEEN ELIZABETH II

There is so little differ-
ence between husbands,
you might as well keep
the first.
—ADÉLÉ ROGERS ST. JOHN

Children

We are all born rude. No infant has ever appeared yet with the grace to understand how inconsiderate it is to disturb others in the middle of the night.
—Judith Martin

Even when freshly washed and relieved of all obvious confections, children tend to be sticky.
—Fran Lebowitz

The most effective form of birth control I know is spending the day with my kids.
—Jill Bensley

i know how to
do anything—i'm
a mom.

—ROSEANNE ARNOLD

It sometimes happens, even in the best of families, that a baby is born. This is not necessarily cause for alarm. The important thing is to keep your wits about you and borrow some money.

—ELINOR GOULDING SMITH

A successful parent is one who raises a child who grows up and is able to pay for her or his own psychoanalysis.

—NORA EPHRON

We want far better reasons for having children than not knowing how to prevent them.

—DORA RUSSELL

Parents of young children should realize that few people, and maybe no one, will find their children as enchanting as they do.

—BARBARA WALTERS

Oh, to be only half as wonderful as my child thought I was when he was small, and only half as stupid as my teenager now thinks I am.

—REBECCA RICHARDS

Youth and Age

This is a youth-oriented society, and the joke is on them because youth is a disease from which we all recover.

—Dorothy Fuldheim

Nature gives you the face you have at twenty; it is up to you to merit the face you have at fifty.

—Coco Chanel

For years I wanted to be older, and now I am.

—Margaret Atwood

The secret of staying young is to live honestly, eat slowly, and lie about your age.

—Lucille Ball

**I refuse to admit that I am more than fifty-two, even
if that does make my sons illegitimate.**

—LADY NANCY ASTOR

Age is something that doesn't matter, unless you are a cheese.
—Billie Burke

Confusion and Anxiety

One learns in life to keep silent and draw one's own confusions.

—CORNELIA OTIS SKINNER

Today, if you're not confused, you are not thinking clearly.

—IRENE PETER

If you can keep your head when all about you are losing theirs, it's just possible you haven't grasped the situation.

— JEAN KERR

If I knew what I was so anxious about, I wouldn't be so anxious.

—MIGNON MCLAUGHLIN

The Last Word

When you get into a tight place and everything goes against you, till it seems as though you could not hang on a minute longer, never give up then, for that is just the place and time that the tide will turn.

—HARRIET BEECHER STOWE

Winning may not be everything, but losing has little to recommend it.

—DIANNE FEINSTEIN

Acting is not very hard. The most important things are to be able to laugh and cry. If I have to cry, I think of my sex life. And if I have to laugh, well, I think of my sex life.

—GLENDA JACKSON

To be loved is to be fortunate, but to be hated is to achieve distinction.

—Minna Thomas Antrim

I am extraordinarily patient, provided I get my own way in the end.

—Margaret Thatcher

How many cares one loses when one decides not to be something, but to be someone.

—Coco Chanel

There are few nudities so objection-able as the naked truth.

—Agnes Repplier

Never drink black coffee at lunch; it will keep you awake in the afternoon.

—Jilly Cooper

The cure for anything is salt water—sweat, tears, or the sea.

—Isak Dinesen

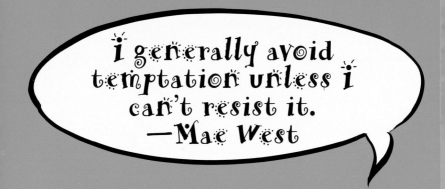